TOUCHED BY ITS *rays*

TOUCHED BY ITS *rays*

poems by Walter Donway

The
ATLAS
SOCIETY
The Center for Objectivism

WASHINGTON, D.C.

Manufacturing by McQuiddy Printing, Nashville, TN
Book design by Laura Deleot, Crookston Design

ISBN 978-0-9815023-0-4 (hardcover)

The Atlas Society
1001 Connecticut Ave., NW, Suite 425
Washington, D.C. 20036
www. atlassociety.org

To Roger Donway

" . . . and should you die
without reaching full sunlight,
you will die on a level
touched by its rays . . . "

—Ayn Rand, *Atlas Shrugged*

CONTENTS

A Prelude

Begin with only this: desire—desire
To do this thing that snatched away my gaze,
When young, and spun it skyward to the fire
They say is great Apollo's gift of days.

I raise my arms, but there is none to see
A man, too old for games, who lofts the bronze
Against the pale Corinthian sky when he
Is all alone, the hour before day dawns.

Ah, how I loved the discus when a lad!
The man as still as marble Herakles,
As though no limb, no muscle, ever had
An end but one: to strike the very skies.

A stirring, then, as if the stone would waken!
The hips begin to twist, the foot advance;
In motions men since games at Troy have taken,
He surges in the spinning, sacred dance!

The gods love men who win the *agones*.
I felt Nemea's call, but did not go.
To train like that a boy so poor agrees
To wager life upon a single throw.

WALTER DONWAY

For me, Apollo's dawn is just as bright
Today, the discus smooth upon my skin,
The breeze upon my nakedness as light
As if the gods were murmuring: Begin!

Now, all I am must flow into these hands;
I gaze as from some inner eye and see
Not cliffs, nor waves below, nor salt-white sands,
But just that moment when the disc flies free.

Perhaps one day this discus could be hurled
From those great cliffs that rise above the beach,
And fly the ceaseless winds that whip the world
To seas and shores that I will never reach.

Though none recall the man, the deed, the time,
A boy, just glancing up in future days,
To read the hour in the sun's slow climb,
May see my discus, flashing in its rays.

Touched By Its Rays

To Ethan

It is my role, surely, ever has been,
To dry the tears, to say the pain will pass:
A little rain, just now, and sunshine, then.
The bump, that stubborn button, the lemonade
That never seemed to sell, the awful fever
Waylaying our vacation, the Band Aid
Appalling to pull: Your hero foretold
That, as these came, so they would go, secure
In hope you could not share, and ever bold
To beard the lion.

                But, today, my son,
You do not cry. When you have loved and lost,
Possessing, knowing, ruling all—then none—
You weep, and weep in pain that's yours alone.
No seasoned glance assesses its depth
And fixes the compass on shores well-known.
My nostrums, packets of sagacity,
Reside like tired toys in some shuttered past.
In this pain you are a stranger to me.
Where is the infant's familiar distress,
The child's toppled pride crying for the kiss?

I might pose that life goes on. I could guess
A clear day may come to dry tears, and let
A laugh gust past the heart's rage, and love—
Not mine, not pills from that old cabinet—
Redress your soul's nakedness. Oh, may it be.
May you become the father to the child,
Though that be all, all that remains of me.

Knowing You
(For Robin)

I lift the blanket.
Your skin feels like a gift warmed
By the giver's hands.

Amid many scents
From your bath, I sniff your hair
And there I find you.

In your taste I read
The recollection of seas,
The salt pools at dawn.

Your wakening sigh
Is like the swish of the sheets
That you push aside.

In the candle light
Your hands lie still at your sides
Though my gaze is long.

When She Is Lonely

Selena walks by the sea when she is lonely.
Selena walks when the day is dawning,
Selena walks through the golden pools of morning.

Selena's white robe from her shoulders goes slipping,
Slipping and falling as she is walking,
And far now and small as Selena goes striding.

O Selena is naked, but there's no one to see,
No one to see that white skin is golden,
That gold hair so whitens, as she strides in the sun.

There's no one to see that Selena is running,
Splashing up diamonds the sun casts away,
As the low waves go reaching so far up the sand.

There's no one to hear that Selena is crying,
Cries of a seabird so far from the land,
The swift silent stalkers so closely pursuing.

They're leaping and splashing through silvery pools;
She is fleeing, her slim legs outstretching,
And her glistening breasts now rising and falling.

So warm in the sun are the pools where she's lying;
Her cries of a seabird none now can hear.
All naked, Selena's white body is twisting.

All over her body the sly hands are sliding,
Seeking and seizing secrets so tender.
Her twisting is ceaseless as the uncurling surf.

Selena is still, and the hands are caressing,
Fingers that tease as breezes go kissing.
And no one is seeing Selena's small smiling.

O Selena is walking, walking and dreaming;
No one can hear Selena's sweet singing.
Selena walks by the sea when she is lonely.

WALTER DONWAY

La Petite Mort

"Come see this golden bird," I said.
You dried the pots, and essayed, then,
To press against my back to look
At where my golden bird had been.

"Just listen, dear, what Keats writes here,"
I called to you. And, yes, you came,
After you phoned your sis and mom,
But Keats somehow was not the same.

I see now in the bathroom doorway
Your beautiful nude silhouette,
A still life framed forever there,
Deliberate at your toilette.

And over me has come a cool
Blue stillness of the blood; I lie
And muse that Plato celebrated
This moment when the passions die.

For you does time change nothing—
The real held forever bright
In heaven's static radiance,
As still as deer surprised by light?

Or do we live from pulse to pulse,
Persisting in synaptic blips
That blend as in a motor's hum
That tickles on the fingertips?

It is the self lives pulse to pulse—
And living, knows that life goes by;
And I descry, in moments missed,
A being left alone to die.

Double Exposure

My dear, last night I had that dream
Of walking naked through the mall,
Where people pass but never seem
To notice my affront at all.
In my dream, I have the thought:
I must be mad, this cannot be!
I'm suffering, as like as not,
An idée fixe on nudity.
Or else, I dream, to my relief,
I'm lying fast asleep in bed,
The victim of (I hope) a brief
Brain-cell disturbance in my head.
But still, I wonder when I'll see
You naked in the dream with me.

Complications

Come praise Apollo bright,
Who prickled a thick brow,
Briefly as lambent light:

Sufficient though to cause
A remorseless shuffling
Across dry plains to pause;

Instinctual eyes
Lift from predator, prey,
To puzzle at vacant skies;

Behind a brutish face,
Unfathomable
Complexity to take place.

WALTER DONWAY

Above Tiananmen Square

At first, we wonder why the square
Appears deserted, knowing that scores
Or more had fought and fallen there,
And guess the camera has not shown
The panicked faces glancing back
To where one man now stands alone.

The crowd may clamor with voices
Of warning; but perhaps for him
The moment passed for making choices.
He stands like one arrayed in ranks
To blunt the insensate lunge
Of those preposterous tanks.

Seeing but thin shoulders, askew
With his incongruous bundles,
Who can tell us if he knew
That great deeds irritate our age,
Which inters them in pearls of glory
To spare us inconvenient rage?

Try to Remember

How many knew, that day,
That we had buried her,
Untenderly, the way
The violated lady
Once asked to seek
Merciful obscurity?

Oh, she had been lovely.
She dared all who would see
To hope that life again
Might be as young, as new,
As the hearts of boys when
Their secret dreams are green.

So bountiful, and she
Was big and easy, too;
And because she was free
Drew so many to her side.
Her head was held so high:
Around her, only the sea,
Above her, only the sky.
They ever failed who sought
To take her; so many sons
To keep her free had fought
Two centuries of wars.

WALTER DONWAY

Evil came stealthily
That morning, like the heart
That festers with envy.
Who spied the swooping blow
That ravished utterly,
Swift and obscene to know
What was untouchable?
Bickering, strutting through
Corridors of power,
Disposed for the eye: Who
That day was by her side—
That world men once called "new"?

An Ayn Rand Centennial

(b. 1905, St. Petersburg)

Philosophy saves us one mind at a time,
Or not at all, and only by our choice.
You knew that, witnessing the master crime
That spawned our century and set man's voice
To amplifying assent. The very mind
Resounded like a sanctum overthrown
By mere bedazzled savages, purblind
To all that private man had made his own.

The altar of our age is politics:
For heaven, power; for sanctity, the plan
To end all plans; and prayerful edicts
To fashion forth the perfect good of man.
How could they bear to hear your lonely voice
Summoning us before that honest bar
Where each alone with reason makes his choice
And pays the price to things as they are?

II

In cities, jungles, mountains, and at sea:
For some, the fighting was their only school,
Their calling to kill for a century
Of brotherhood. To die was merciful:
Idealists spared the bumper crop of death
As socialism swept the world to cleave
Mankind's collective neck, and those still left
Uncertain who the master, who the slave.

 A price in blood unknown in history
Had made us doubt the very human clay,
Abjure ideals, and make philosophy
Of going back. But you arose to say
Two thousand years of tribute to the creed
Of sacrifice, with almsman for our priest—
No hostage held too dear for haughty need—
Had ushered in this hour of the beast.

III

"The world's salvation lies in beauty,"
Said one dark seer, who knew that art compels
Assent beyond mere argument, that we
May know of worlds where catastrophe dwells.
With you we walked through cities once higher
Than sunrise, seeing all we thought our birthright
Brought down because that brash hero with his fire
But earned his awful ledge and endless night.

On the skyline of man's incandescent day
An infinity of brave lights died.
Alone you knew that all was swept away
By festering envy of human pride.
And by what grace, we wondered, could you see
Those cities fade, forsaken by an age,
That famished souls might sate their envy—
Could see, and speak, and yet not die of rage?

IV

The shifting signs of stars could not explain
His birth. The holy men did not declare
His soul redeemed from the immortal stain
(Or come to marvel at his golden hair).
He told us that he lived for joy alone,
His warrant reason's right. And suddenly,
Because a guiltless gaze returned our own,
We knew that he had banished God, and was free.

Behold the man whose soul is no god's grant,
Is not a sojourner on Earth, nor guest
Escorted by the body, nor supplicant.
The Earth is his by right of his conquest.
For nature's stubborn virtue will succumb
To none but men of reason, who can take her
Even within her high, sequestered sanctum.
And of his soul this man alone is maker.

V

Notations never are ideas, which live
In minds when minds are thinking. That day
When you had given all you had to give,
And we became your ideas, none could say
If man would ever elevate the light
Of reason, long tormented and estranged,
Because a score of grateful mortals might
Have comprehended you and been changed.

Yet to remit one tithe of man's distress,
Redeem an age long leached of pity,
Somehow rescind that perplexed emptiness
Engraved upon the sky of freedom's city,
But pay with life and joy, would be a crime.
Does death absolve the prophet for his voice?
Philosophy saves us one mind at a time,
Or not at all, and only by our choice.

Red Rover

O where you have gone, Red Rover?
And do you recall how we bent
To charge the ranks of old idols?
As to a trumpet's cry we went!

We thought to topple every foe:
The labyrinth of faith, the spell
Of antique sin—all the prisons
Of humility where men dwell.

And did you leave the line to seek
The comfort that the world acclaims,
Bestows if one will but forswear
The child's intolerable games?

And do you brood upon that lash
We swore to strike from every hand
That would dispose, as if by right,
What free men built in freedom's land?

For now the public creatures swarm
Our harvests, brazen as vermin;
By night, the dogmas walk again:
To guide us—stars or the sermon.

And was your fate to see it all,
And feel the rage again, Red Rover?
And in your dreams come racing back?
For the battle's still not over.

A Ghost at Yalta

(For George N. Crocker)

Survey with me this mild coast
Edging a hard hinterland.
Sea winds sweeten evening,
Beguiling us to hope that minds
Might be touched by human longing.

Here, in the late winter,
Like tourists on holiday,
Aides with alacrity
Habiting the palaces
Of bygone czars and princes,
Debarked a few aged men:
One sated on power, ill,
Borne to victory astride
A country too young too fail;
One fresh from satanic precincts
Of humanity where men
In millions perished as per plan;
One bred to set relations
Of nations homicidal
But once a generation.

Eight days they gave (starting late,
continuing at banquets)
To parcel out the fate
Of half-a-billion people
Who had endured by dreaming
That after war might be life.
Nations traded, or sundered;
Ancient cities awarded;
Millions pushed across the map
As though Versailles taught nothing;
Elections hung on the pledge
Of a power-mad tyrant;
Toasts upraised to genocide;
Prisoners shipped back to die;
Slave labor for millions sanctioned:
Neither right, nor realm, nor writ
Of law was beyond the favor
Of power and privilege
A crippled man lived to savor.

How shall this shade seek sleep
Who was a Latvian
Bartered across that table?
A German shipped to Russia

As human reparations?
A refugee herded home
To certain execution?
A Polish democrat betrayed
To fifty years of puppet rule?
These and legion others
Sold across that table
In the Crimean winter?
More than half a century
From Berlin to Beijing
We have ever paid the price
For deeds those men did here,
Amid the toasts and feasting,
Who trafficked death, slavery,
And pain but never bore it.

All who marshal history
To annotate their briefs
Demanding justice, tell me:
Where is peace for this spirit
Until the world remembers,
And deeds done here make Yalta
A word men use for evil?

The Prophet

We tell the story, tell it yet again.
A man is born who might be you or me:
This house, that street; the required omen
Affirmed at once, or by posterity;
The child cherished, banished, or set adrift
Upon the merciless ordinary,
To find (or is it not to lose?) his gift.
On how, on when, reports may vary.
In retrospect, we all affirm, his stride,
Although like thunder, none now recalls.
He shared our days: worked, ate, prayed by our side.
But where we saw our lot, within those walls
That teach us who we are, and who our sons
Will be, he saw a servitude beyond
Iniquity, and all our satisfactions
Mere wheedling favors won by those who fawned
Upon oppression. We hung our heads for shame
That one more day might pass, the yoke still worn.
We whispered our despair, it was his name;
We spoke his name aloud, our hope was born.
We followed him, afraid to go, or stay,
And many quarrelsome to hide their doubt.
The forests, deserts, mountains of our way

So wrung the town-bred heart that we would shout:
Return! Return! Some died with that last look
That casts a final, fearful curse. He grieved,
With us, he shed his tears upon the book,
And said, for us, the words we had believed.
Some tell of days, some months, until we gazed
Upon a valley (much like those before,
A few would murmur) and, with hand upraised,
He made the sign that we would search no more.
How we went mad, then, runnning with a will,
And calling loudly, as though we might be met
By crowds. But only we ran down that hill:
To settle, live, and await a prophet.

The Gift

The revolution was the thing
When I was young, until it took
A turn for the worse to hellward.
So then, I cried, let freedom ring;

I'll live for liberty—for dope,
Parades of neo-Nazis, porn,
And the pursuit of happiness.
But freedom was busy selling soap.

I told my love: For only you
I live, and do not weep for me.
But dear, said she, we have to talk,
And...sorry, but...I'll miss you, too.

So then, I sighed: My son, I give
To you the world, my lot and shares;
But thanks, he wasn't having any.
The old, hard voice said: You must live.

Unlawful To Remove

Although each Heart must meet
Exacting specifications,
Regarding product life
We make no representations.

We are not liable
For items locked in Heart
For periods outside ranges
Set forth in nearby chart.

Though storage can discolor,
Blur, or fade some images,
Maker is held harmless
For resulting damages.

Use care when elements
Known to be combustible
Are commingled in the Heart;
Maker is not liable.

The Heart will open easily
With your Personal Password;
Though warranty does not cover
Lost words or the costs incurred.

Maker welcomes comments
Consumers may impart
For new creative uses.
And thanks for choosing Heart.

Yours to Keep
(For Jerome Kagan)

Let us gather now and each unwrap his gift:
For some, the sun, the smile, the ready hand,
For some, the easeful shadow we call shy.
A change in size or other modest shift
May be allowed, but kindly understand
Your gift is yours to keep until you die.

For some, surprise? For some, perhaps, delight?
But parents always doubted it was chance;
And Galen, just two centuries A.D.,
In Athens, had it very nearly right:
Our body's chemistry holds the balance
That makes me sanguine, you melancholy.

And now the weight of evidence compels
With rigor toasted in psychology:
At just four months, though John and Jim don't speak
Or walk, the story that the data tells
Is of a proto-personality—
That John is bold, while Jim is rather meek.

Though Jim may change (or anyway get older),
To tender nerves the world is no less grim:
He's frazzled, guilty, lonely, bruised, and blue.
John's a big boy, too, and growing bolder,
In a world that's never too much with him:
Engaging, avid, in love with the new.

Born in a Land of Opportunity,
Equality being our Apostle's Creed,
We had assumed that shares of contentment,
Like schooling and Social Security,
Were evenly distributed, as guaranteed,
No doubt, in some official document.

No legislative salvation in sight,
However, or pill from the FDA,
We are fated to attend our true birth:
Discover what we are, seek not what might
Have been but what may be, and always pay
The ransom of our soul to know its worth.

Just Wondering

A fellow won a Nobel Prize
For showing that we synthesize
Our memories from proteins.
If you'll excuse my French, that means
My memory of you is meat—
The sort that delis sell to eat.
The godly hold this is not so:
Between our ears or just below
There dwells a spirit, or a ghost,
Who's said to have arrived almost
Exactly when the egg met sperm
And won't depart till flesh meets worm.
In favor of this startling view?
All knowledge absent, it will do.
Across the aisle, with equal zeal,
They claim that just the meat is real.
Reflect a moment, they insist,
That mind's a spook; it can't exist.
But would a trillion bytes of stuff,
All syncopating, be enough
To swirl around the letters here
And feel a moment's hope or fear?

How It Was

I had forgotten how to write of love,
Of hair as dark as clouds in May, or hair
As yellow as the poets say; above,
A face that is—what phrase?—ah, more than fair;
And breasts so pert in pink that words go blind.
All that once stopped me, stiff as Perseus
Had he no trick of putting things behind.
Yet, now it seems no more than youthful fuss
About new models coming in '08:
The contours great, how nice a drive would be!
But then, amidst an evening's passionate,
Preposterous chatter, you smiled at me
Across a table, spoke your quiet thought;
And anyhow brown hair, brown glasses, too,
Like things that I had known, but long forgot,
Were writing poems that I would give to you.

WALTER DONWAY

Seven Callers Waiting

I know I said I'd give a ring—
And would—except that anything
At all that I can think to say
Reminds you what you ate today.

It's true, I haven't phoned you, yet.
With all your little ways so set
I fear an unexpected call
Might jar an etching off your wall.

Well, yes, I rarely get in touch.
Of late, your politics are such
That with each argument we've had
I'm more inclined to think you mad.

All right, I know how long I've stalled;
I swear, it was last spring you called!
The fact is, though, I still can't face
A weekend at your summer place.

I have not called in four years, now.
(Your insult left me asking how.)
Insisting you were right makes worse
Your feral alcoholic curse.

A friend must call a friend—I know.
I took your number, card, and—oh,
But how frank can a fellow be
When it's your accent bothers me?

My cherished friend—for you, alone,
I reach with pleasure for my phone.
Why, before you've read this e-mail through
I may be on the line to you!

WALTER DONWAY

Party Animal

Prescribe for me the etiquette
Of parties in Hampton gardens
On August evenings when sunset
Conjures magical motionless deer.
I must not stand alone and gaze
To where the mist dissolves the field
So that the deer seem to appraise
Our world as from a world apart.
I must not fix on sunburnt limbs,
Or brown breasts with ghostly straps,
Nor wander off when talking dims
No more the bygone, beckoning arms.
My conversation must not dare
Invade thought's sanctum or abash
A tender, blushing bosom where
Perhaps an idea may reside.
With drink my addled tongue might name
The wealth full faithfully displayed;
Or might, insensible to shame,
Refer to war (or even God).
Tell me, that I may learn how late
And easy days of summer laugh,
Or learn, at last, it is my fate
To gaze as from a world apart.

Atlas Shrugged: The Fiftieth Anniversary

The invocation is to none but me,
Calling upon no god, or star, or ashes,
Annointing no history or prophecy.

I am the sanction, the man who came
Alone and naked to the world's golden rim
To raise my arms, to see, and speak a name.

Mine is the name. I have looked upon Earth;
And none can name for me what is.
I am alone at reason's birth.

At this altar, no sacrifice, no knee bent;
I have scaled the mountains of my freedom
To bring to you a single mind's assent.

A farm in New England; an old white barn;
Two boys who roam until the moon has slipped
Above the woods to frost the fields and ponds;
The Sunday steeples rising as in prayer
For creeds that once had writhed in holy fire;
The house, its rooms adrift with books, like fields
New cut for reaping in their season:

Two boys, still beardless, sit on worn stone steps,
Or lie beneath the eaves, to read one book—
And know the world is theirs to make.

 Just say it was our destiny,
As immigrants who chose
No legacy save liberty,
To fall in love with heroes.

But with a continent to build,
What did free men have to do
With swords, and plumes, and castles filled
With grain that peasants grew?

Who would define for us the man
Who dared all upon the sea,
Who saw that here the world began,
And dreamed of what would be?

He made his mark from coast to coast;
It's called the blesséd land.
For thanks, they scourged him at the post
And burned him with the brand.

So he carried on, defiant—
But wondered why he should.
The honest called him "giant"—
None knew to call him "good."

But we were witness to the birth
Of truth—and O, the glory—
As men whose genius won the Earth
Rose to hear their story.

And now it's half a century
That I have said: Francisco,
Rearden, Ragnar, Galt, and Dagny—
Always their names just so.

All born for me in one instant,
As real as any friend,
Alive in realms so radiant
The eye can see no end.

Empire of Earth

I drop this sweet thick soil, but it clings
In creases of my hand, upraised against
The glaring, shoreless seas of prairie grass,
Where two bright blades of steel thrust to the west.

A half a continent—a decade, too—
Will take you back to where the cities end,
And I began. It's where the wagon trains
Are white threads tugged off the urban skein
And woven westward by an unseen hand.
Where horse and mule and man took up their loads
For the lurching first steps west, I stood
And saw two lines converging at the sky—
A royal highway of geometry
On which the many thousands gathered there
Might cross desert, plain, and mountain range
As easily as Chinese emperors rode!

Two years I scouted, then rode off the plains
To take my dream to money men of myth
Within the hushed cathedrals of Chicago's
Mighty banks. I felt their frowning study,
Their glances at my beard, and clothes, and hands.
I might have been some missionary priest,

All scarred and bronzed by years in jungle climes,
Returned to witness he had done God's work.
Bishops in silken robes, amidst the gold,
The incense, and the priceless tapestries,
But half attended with arch, incurious smiles.
I wove in words and spelled upon the air
What I myself had seen: the prairie loam
Erupting crops of spring and winter wheat;
The timber stands streaming like nomad nations
From the western mountain face to Puget Sound.
And then: Pacific passage!

                    The bankers stared
And sighed and shrugged—patiently instructed me
That empty land unfolds a thousand miles
Where town and farm and mine are all unknown.
They deigned to teach me what my eyes had seen,
Describing places I myself had trod,
With snowshoes skimming seas of drifting white
In mountain passes that the old wolf shuns.

Go east, they said, go east, and try your line
Up marble steps that rise at easy grade
To halls of Congress, where one may win

Dominions vaster than the tsars could covet.
No need, they said, to speak of trains and freight,
For there you may hold forth to bankers
Beholden to no savers, risking gold
They did not earn and do not reckon dear.
Such men could wave their pens and make it pay
To push my tracks across the barren plains,
Through notches cut like letters on the sky,
And down to forests distant as the moon.

But I would have no part of it, no halls
Where rail is laid on paper, and the land
Is staked on tablecloths, and each day dawns
Upon more worthless shares, more bonds, more loans.
I do not lay my steel on ground the gift
Of public men who at a stroke dispose
A million acres they have never seen.
The day that men who live upon this land
Decline my clasp to seal my right to pass
That day forever will be end-of-steel.

So I rode west and never east again.
I pressed my track into the yielding earth,
Beneath the weight of trains of immigrants,

Until new towns rose up on either side.
And harder then I pressed as trains rolled west.
I did not rush unfurling measured miles
To harvest crops of subsidies and grants.
The bankers in Chicago murmured: "Folly."
But now I had my advocates in tolling bells
That rang the passing trains from church to church.

Three nights ago, I tarried in a town
New-built beside the track, like hundreds more,
Each with its grip upon this line of steel
Like climbers on a parlous mountain side.
Here were a dozen earthen prairie homes,
A trading shack still open to the air,
A blacksmith at his bench beneath the sky:
All plans, and talk, and work, and boasts, and hopes.
That night we feasted, danced, and drank the hale
Of the tiny town. And the eyes of girls
And the grins of lads are ever the same
Where the work is hard and the hope is high.
And suddenly voices and friendly hands
Were pushing me into the firelight, with cheers
And claps as though this were some jubilee.
I turned and saw those faces framed in light

As from a vision shimmering on air
Above the dark prairie. For they beheld
A dream as bright as rose for me one day.
No words escaped the fist that held my heart.

At dawn, the engine's steady, patient gasps
Raised swirling skirts of cloud about its knees;
The whistle loosed its iron moan to hills
That rolled it round the wakening plains.
And every man, and woman, some with babes,
Looked up to where I stood, and at their backs
The rising sun swept to the unknown West.

Tonight, we make our camp at end-of-steel
Where high plains surge against the mountains
And break, retreat; but we push on at dawn.
On every trail are straining mules and men:
Surveyors first, on trail I broke and blazed
Long since; and then cutters, blasters, bedders,
All squalling Irish, Dutch, and Chinaman;
Then engineers and masons brace the cuts
And trim the gorges with majestic trestles.

Touched By Its Rays

By some good grace it is not ours to see
The full price that is set upon our dreams.
A thousand miles behind Red River bridge,
Was where a stranger rashly saw this day.
A stranger, yes, for what of his is mine?
I have a hand half stubs of fingers,
A face the hue of cedar turned to weather,
A beard as bleached as chalk-white trailside bones.
Out of my little shard of looking glass
Stare blue eyes as stormed as mountain winter.
The doctors say that only dead men know
Such wounds as scar my chest. And memory
Tells tales to awe that stranger who was me:
How we would madly throw down tools and grasp
For guns when Indian war cries slit the air.

I mean to have my way in this fair land:
Traveling to the ocean shore on trains
That roar like Odin through the forest pines;
Dispatching swaying boxcars full of wheat
To hungry millions for their daily bread;
Piling high the sawmills' planks of lumber
On flatcars bound for harbors, and Cathay;
And raising factories for the handiwork
Unguessed that is the genius of free men.

WALTER DONWAY

These visions crowd like friends about the fires
I keep in lonely camps too cold for sleep.
But I pretend no easy prophecy.
We live in sky, but walk upon the land;
And I will spike my dreams into the Earth.

Enough for Sunday Morning

All slides along the tilting deck
As reason's very stitching tears,
What comes still shapeless in the fog;
A time is coming for nightmares.

Today, just sun on cobblestones,
Fall friendly in the little street,
Sweet sighing from the bakery,
A bench outside, and one more seat.

In Cortona

Another hill, another town upthrust
As though this Tuscan earth must toss, must lie
Unsleeping, twist and pull its bunching crust,
Expose at last a bared hip to the sky;

Another church, erected where streets cross,
Bestride life's noon—rude, placid, assured that we,
At last, at this sheer face, will own our loss
Is utter and will beg for clemency:

But now I know I cannot enter, here,
Approach another altar notable
For craftsmanship or lift my eyes to peer
At arches (Roman, of local marble).

I wave the others in, but wait; for me,
No church abides behind this storied wall,
No spirit haunts the treasured reliquary
To soften ancient hurts the scenes recall.

Could I for just an hour enter, know
What shudder flung this weight at heaven's face
And gathered all that labor could bestow—
Of beauty, hope, rejoicing—to this place?

I turn at last to steps the Tuscan sky
Has warmed, where children sit and face away
To watch the crowds of tourists flock to buy
Their fancies. I am happy for this day.

A Dialogue of Fear and Love

FEAR   A moonlit errand to the barn, its loft
A cyclops eye, and the wind hissing Run:
The boy could have tried to rally the line,
But the story is fear, all said and done.
Fear is the theme.

LOVE   A dreamer like that boy
Will share the night with jinns and they will be
As real to him as pegs. But when he dreams,
He casts his nets upon the rimless sea
Of possibility, where heroes sail
Before the mast. A boy like that will read
And fall in love—and love's the story, here.

FEAR   Oh, Tarzan, Sherlock Holmes: One hardly need
Review that troop, which, for a fleeting season,
Will stride through realms that spill a golden light
On children's faces in our world. The boy
Imagined he could set against the night
A day that breaks on lands that never were.

Touched By Its Rays

LOVE The future is a land that never was.
What but love creates that land? For fear
Repels and nothing more. You won't deny
That boy was one who used the stars to steer.
The first to speak for him is *Atlas Shrugged*,
That vision that redeemed the joy of man,
And dashed the shackles from Prometheus.
In those pages, a fierce love began.

FEAR He saw so much of possibility,
And knew the hero in us must not die.
And yet, he lived a hostage to his fear.
The boy an autumn night could terrify
Became the man whose genius could discern
The dawn of his deliverance, and know
It rose upon the valley of the heroes,
The homeland of his longing, and yet bow,
And turn, unwilling to ascend the mountains
Of his fear.

LOVE Against one mark you stand
Mankind, but each man with his fear's alone
And knows the cost in courage he has paid.
In forty years or more, has any known
This man to cry the garrison must fall,

Stand down the lonely vigils he has kept,
Or leave the ancient marches to the foe?
He tenders love that fair men will accept.

FEAR He did the bidding of the world, a mouse
Of offices, with whispering steps that seem
To press the years into the granite stairs—
A mouse who ever nursed the eagle's dream.
Come, pity him the fear that is himself.
A fear can slip into the heart, as cold
As if the alien grave had spoken;
With hands outcast like hooks, for any hold,
A man may miss the sticking place, and fear
Has made a slave.

LOVE   I pity only fear,
Which never looked in eyes that light the mind
And saw assent. Long years ago, fear lost
That man in the still moments that find
Us each alone with reason and the world.
But even now we glimpse fear's face above;
The window dims the strumpet's grimace!
Sad whore! You beckon to a man in love.

Touched By Its Rays

Letter to His Son

Just now I watched the evening fill our street,
The black submerge all built or known or dear.
It caught me there and swirled about my feet
And rose around to choke me in my fear.

Today, I heard about a man I know
Who found his son, a high-school boy, they said—
Exactly how—and this a week ago—
But in the tub was where he was, and dead.

From heroin, they said, an overdose.
Now telling gets a little hard for me
Because the telling lets it come so close:
But yes, his school was where you used to be.

How much like guilt the common things will weigh.
I eat my toast and ponder how my friend
Can hope to live this minute or this day:
"But we will lunch though worlds and eras end."

You should not think, so seldom do I write,
This comes but from your troubles at that school—
Admitting, though, as darkness rose tonight
A ghastly shape seemed bobbing on that pool.

WALTER DONWAY

Bat

Little mad mouse face,
Old glove on a nail,
In a lightless place;

Small furred bird of night,
Eyeless aerialist,
In your prescribed flight:

In our screams you hear,
Across ancient dusks,
Our blood's antique fear

Ever clothed anew
In tales, round our fires,
of evil you do.

Viking Woman

(For Pink Snow)

War god, why have you taken my love?
I know you hear the warrior's cries,
And covet the bravest,
And choose who lives or dies.

Come, I want no other man.
Come, take me if you can.

One man who sacred strode cathedral groves,
One man who radiant rode the sea,
And godless knelt on heights,
That man alone could take me.

Come, I want no other man.
Come, take me if you can.

War god, why have you taken my love?
You ever have craved the bravest one,
Relished the defiant cry,
Of him who will not run.

Come, I want no other man.
Come, take me if you can.

WALTER DONWAY

For whose wild grasp can strip these pressing breasts,
Or force apart these thighs he knew,
Ride this valley of desire
As but one man could do?

Come, I want no other man.
Come, take me if you can.

My spirit does not pine for paradise,
For ecstasies the soul may lack,
Or dreams distilled of mists:
Just Earth beneath my back.

Come, I want no other man.
Come, take me if you can.

But know I wield the sword my lover wore,
Will kill you as you killed my man,
The only one knew me.
Come, take me if you can.

A Sense of Life

Right in this room I caught her, yes; its strange,
The cliff so close, all dark, just yards away.
Would you go bounding over rocks the moon
Makes treacherous—that battering surf below?
From that, I guessed this side the safer one,
But had scant fear, in any case—the house
So far above the highroad that its lights
Were dots to any thief or band of brigands.
The war had left nowhere to live, no food;
To stay at home was much the choice to starve.
The girl—I'll get to her—looked like a lad
But for her breasts, and hips, perhaps: all bone
And hair from eating only twice a week.
But none of that, you see, had touched me,
Back then, with gold and foreign scrip to spare,
And left alone by all authorities:
My father died a hero in the war.
I look back, now: so many struggling,
But I was almost going mad each day
With painting canvases as stiff and lifeless
As those poor corpses mornings by the road.

WALTER DONWAY

That day—oh, fifteen years ago—I worked
Till twilight in this room. And in my soul.
Infernal fealty to the style and school
Adored in Paris, then, and Rome, which viewed
The world as through some shattered spectacles,
Had hobbled me for years. So much success
So young: Adoring critics, and salons, too,
Had left me but to long for that lost glory.
From this dim room, I gazed upon the cliffs
Where red sun rimmed the rocks, and redder rays
Still shot up from the sea, and thought of death:
To die like Shelley, Byron, some mad thing.
The French say though that sleep's "the little death,"
And that was good enough for me that night.

The sleep of wine is deep enough, but short.
I woke covered in that unearthly white
With which the moon will tug you to a window.
Await the breaking of a dreaded day?
I went instead to see if I had left
A bit of wine in the carafe or glass.
Atop the stairs in slippers, robe, I paused:
A sound–a slipping catch, perhaps? Or what?
Years back most all with money kept a gun.

Touched By Its Rays

Quite bristling like a wakened hound, I fetched it.
With what relief I yielded up to fear.
Let mercy dash my life beyond repair!

Two long flights down I reached my studio.
Now! I swerved to stand within the doorway,
My gun stuck out, and in the moonlit room
A shadow leaped like a great black cat.
With singing nerves I cried and fired, then,
But not before my brain had broadcast: girl!
Did that perhaps deflect my aim an inch
And thereby flick the axis of my world?

She halted with a cry—the shot did that.
The French doors cast a silver slanting light.
Her eyes went round in that near-wasted face.
Alarm was there, and fear, but such a look
As said: I want to understand before I die.
Aloud, she said: "I came to steal some food—
Some food or money—or I'm going to starve."
It's then I flipped the switch and saw her;
She faced me, shapeless in her hanging rags,
And said no more, awaiting what I'd say.
I waved the gun. "This way." She stepped ahead.

One flight up, I sat her in the kitchen
And put before her all my odds and ends
Of food that one eats cold, a quick buffet.
She glanced up, said nothing, started to eat.
It's then it hit: a notion that just seized
My mind—and I suppose changed everything.
That bony face gone gaunt with starving,
The eyes unnaturally large, the uncut hair
A flowing golden frame: Hers seemed to me
A beauty scarcely for this Earth. And yet,
And yet...a starving girl, a gun on her,
Sat dining like a countess all at ease.
She raised her eyes to meet my gaze. I swear
I saw a smile, elusive as a whisper,
Saluting life's grand talent for surprise.
I said: "You won't like meeting our police.
You won't if you will stay here for awhile."
She shook her head, still eating, and replied:
"I can't," as though I'd asked her out to lunch.
"Just use me now, tonight, and then I go."
"Not far. Police out here are very fast."
"But maybe you won't want me more than once."
I felt so odd a brew of jealousy
And anger that I cried: "No, no. I paint..."

"I know." "You do?" "The turpentine I smelled."
"I want to paint you. Seems you have no choice."
She stared at me, again—that wondering look,
As though Magician Life had done a trick.
"No choic ," she said, her child's eyes grave, but then:
"Of course, I might just leap at you, and die.
I have that choice." "Well, choose to live," I said.
I waved the gun. "Your room is there. My dad
Once called that room the 'vault.' She walked to it.
I fetched a tray with all the food she'd left,
And when she took it, closed and locked the door.

I woke, but lay unmoving: What was wrong?
Not wrong, just somehow different. My God!
I actually wanted to get up!
To paint. Paint her? To paint the world she saw.
It was a world I'd known too long ago.

"You didn't want to paint the rags, did you?"
I had unlocked her door and opened it.
She wore my mother's scarlet silk kimono.
She might have been some royal captive,
The way she stood, a concubine princess,
Whose eyes possessed the world she looked upon.

"No, not in rags," I said. "You've eaten more,
So come," and she walked past me to the stairs.
"The studio?" she asked. "Or cliffs," I said.

The morning light made glorious the studio's
French doors that framed the black rock cliffs and sea.
She turned to me. "Now take that off," I said.
"I want you nude." She made no move. I waited,
Then went to her and drew the belt. Her gaze
Was on the sea. Nor did she move as gently
I lifted the kimono open, back,
Across her shoulders, let it fall. She bent,
Took up the garment, held it out, frowned,
Deliberately folded it just so
And laid it on a chair. "Okay," she said,
So low I barely heard, and languidly,
The slowness rendering her every step
A frozen frame to linger in the mind,
She walked around the studio. She paused
Before each canvas as a woman dressed
In evening wear might stroll a gallery.
I snatched my pad and charcoal, sketching her
In lines that curved and turned with her movements,
Although I knew on canvas must be what

Was in her face, was in her eyes; but no,
Must be somehow the world that those eyes saw.

Just once, she neared as though to view my work;
I only shook my head. She turned, but said,
A gesture slicing through my canvases:
"You hardly need a model to paint those."
"No more of that," I said, and knew I spoke
For now and for an interrupted love
That once I hoped to share with all the world,
A love I must redeem, whatever years
Remained to me: that world the soul—and art—
Discern behind hypnotic, unrelenting
Images that pulse upon the mind
From shifting compass points of place and time.

That day I settled on a pose for her
Upon a great rock high above the sea.
She sat, her chin just raised as though she saw
Beyond the frame a world her spirit knew.
She might have been some genius of the Earth,
Her realm below, except no line, no bone,
No angle of her body would suggest
A pleasured favorite of earthly bounty.

WALTER DONWAY

This being battled at the verge of life
And by her love endured to see this day.

Two days we worked. We caught the early light,
But when the sun beat fiercely she would rise
And wordless take the steep long rocky path
That twisted to the beach below. She went
All naked, taking nothing, and when the sun
Relented she returned. She said no word
After her little greeting wave and smile.
We worked again till fading light; she saw
I made false starts, and once began anew,
But did not try to see my work, though once
She said: "There's someone I remind you of."
"Not someone, but a sense that I had once,
A sense, a feeling, for what life might hold."
"That never changes." "No, but one forgets,
Or puts that sense away like childhood toys."
She nodded silently, but later said:
"You wonder how it can survive some things."

Each day, at dusk, we stopped; we ate again.
She quietly went to her room, but I
Long wondered if she slept, or read, or bathed.

Late afternoon on our third day, I stopped,
Just looking at my work and wondering:
Could I have been creator of this thing?
I'd never done or dreamed of art like this.
Intent, I noticed nothing till she stood
Close by my side and said: "It's finished, now."

What startled me was seeing she was right.
I turned, but she was walking toward the path.
She glanced back, then, and waved me after her.
I made the painting safe and walked behind,
Watching the light that slid across her back,
Her hips, her hair, her gently swinging arms.
I reached the sand and saw her waiting smile,
And then a wide, insinuating grin.
This girl, so beautiful, had worn no clothes
For three whole days and suddenly I found
Myself intensely modest standing there.
Hands on hips she waited, watching me,
No mercy, now, as I undid my belt.
When I stood nude she studied me, then laughed,
And turning, ran and dove into the sea.
We bathed and swam; no surf disturbed the calm.
I turned to see her standing on the beach,

Atop her head a sprawling wig of kelp
As long and black and snaky as Medusa.
"No!" I yelled, instinctively, as though I saw
Three days into the past and what I'd felt.
She seized the kelp and slowly, arm far back,
She flung it high and far into the sea.
She sat, then lay, upon the sand. I came,
Stood over her; she only looked at me.
But when I knelt an easing drifted
Through her limbs and I leaned over her.
She raised her arms a little, spreading them.

Cliff shadows crept across us when I asked,
In drowsy whispers: "What's your name?" "Marie,"
She said, "and yours?" "Its Jean, and Jean loves you."
"Of course," she said. "Because it's like the art.
You want someone because you want their world."
"You love their world," I said. "You love their world,
That's true," she said, "you love the world together."
She rose and naked still turned to the path.
Some shock at what I'd done, for three days, now,
Made me call out: "It's chill, please wear my clothes."
She shook her head, still walking, and I followed.
At dinner, wrapped in the kimono, she talked

About the painting, propped now on a chair.
She seemed to think and talk of only it;
Though I was wild to talk of her, of us.
Together at her bedroom door, I said:
"You won't leave, now. You know that I love you?"
She brushed my face. "That's for tomorrow, yes."
She closed the door, but then she said through it:
"Don't lock me, please. I want to swim at dawn."

I'd never sleep, I thought, and thinking it,
I slept and slept, till noon sun baked my back.
I smiled, and nude went down the stairs, but saw
Her door ajar, and calling, heard no sound.
By climbing to the cliff's far lip I saw
The beach and ocean in the noonday sun,
Deserted as the sun-blanched, birdless sky.
As I walked to the house, I called again.
And, well, you know that she had gone, of course,
For all this happened fifteen years ago.
No, that is not the painting. Yes, it's her,
I painted that when she'd been gone a week.
Oh yes, they say that it's a masterpiece—
Perhaps because I'm famous, now. And yet,
It's nothing to compare with that first one,
The painting that she took the day she left.

WALTER DONWAY

The New Muse

Behold the poetry machine,
With whirling blades to shred a scene,
With triple blower jets to free
The fragments of reality.
What of the poet's flights of thought?
Just ask a bird the blades have caught.

Naked: A Play in Verse

Persons In Play
TROUBADOUR
FIRST REPORTER
SECOND REPORTER
JULIETTE JUSTINE
FIRST GUARD
SECOND GUARD
WOMAN FROM THE CROWD
MAN FROM THE CROWD
SECOND WOMAN

On the far left is a black limousine. On the far right in the distance is the entrance to a prison. Facing the audience, the crowd stands at the back of the walkway to the prison. At the front of the stage two reporters stand with microphones. Also at the front left stands the troubadour with his guitar. He plays softly as he speaks his lines and through the play gradually moves from far left to right.

Guards help a handcuffed woman out of the limousine. She is tall and beautiful, with a striking figure. She stands and walks with alluring grace. The guards just behind hold her arms.

TROUBADOUR. It's morning in America
Where free men have arisen
To savor how a goddess
Endures her walk to prison.

FIRST REPORTER. Look now, look now! Look what we have here!
She steps into the sun with all that grace
That won her fame in films that millions loved.
We knew the awe once felt for gods, the longings
Stirred by goddesses.

SECOND REPORTER.   Our camera pans
That vaunted shape as she surveys the crowd.

FIRST REPORTER. This crowd may seek some sign she feels the shame
And pain of her disgrace, a shame not shown
In all her fall from glamor, fame, and wealth.

SECOND REPORTER. It's Juliette Justine, untouchable
Celebrity and Tinsel Town princess.
As she became an idol of the screen
Her privacy became a legend, too.

FIRST REPORTER. How that has changed! My, yes! It changed the night
Last year narcotics agents—newsmen, too—
Invaded private grounds of her estate
And searched the famous guests around the pool.
No drugs were found, but agents did charge two
With violations, later dropped, and they
Became the witnesses against Justine.

SECOND REPORTER. Prosecutors said that she seduced that night
A man—a boy—who may have been sixteen.
First-ever photographs of her estate
Flashed round the globe and millions viewed the bed
Where they made love.

FIRST REPORTER.   The world stop turning, then,
To watch the trial of Juliette Justine
For statutory rape.

TROUBADOUR. A lady sailed across my sky,
And tossing back my head to see
I knew no other lady could
Light up the sky that way for me.

SECOND REPORTER. But Ms Justine
Declined to take the stand, disdained to speak.

FIRST REPORTER. Justine would never help police to find
The unnamed lover, who had disappeared.

SECOND REPORTER. Her trial unleashed a holocaust of rage
About abuse of adolescents.

FIRST REPORTER. About Justine's avoidance of the public,
And all the obligations of her wealth.

SECOND REPORTER. About the secret life of sensual delight
Some say she led.

FIRST REPORTER. And flaunting of restraint
In movies millions of our youth have seen.

SECOND REPORTER. Convicted, she refused to show remorse.

FIRST REPORTER. Apologize, affirm our family values.

SECOND REPORTER. Or even ask for leniency.

FIRST REPORTER.   And so
            Today Justine begins a ten-year term
            In this notorious women's prison.

TROUBADOUR. And then I sang to know true love:
            We grant this tribute to the great.
            But if a mortal rise too high
            Can we distinguish love from hate?

SECOND REPORTER. She's coming, now. The crowd begins to shout.
            A woman cries, "Let's make her walk in naked!"
            A man is yelling, "Strip her, strip her, now!"
            They all take up the cry.

FIRST REPORTER.   The guards shrink back.
            Justine seems not to hear; she gazes now
            To where the great dark walls like tidal waves
            Dwarf the human form. What does she feel?

            A woman steps forth from the crowd. The guards halt, holding
            Justine back.

WOMAN. You see! She's still too proud to notice us!

Justine turns as though seeing the crowd for the first time.

JUSTINE. I always thought of you, and everyone
Who saw my films. For I became an actress
To dream with you what people could become.
I let you dream with me a life of joy
And see it might be possible to you.

WOMAN. We loved to dream an hour away in darkness
But had to know you didn't live that dream—
To know you bickered, cried, got drunk, had pets,
Had humble parents in some little town,
Got fat, and spent obscene amounts on clothes.
You kept all that from us.

JUSTINE. But I kept faith
In life with what I strove to show in art.

WOMAN. You didn't let us leave the dream behind
For gritty jobs and loveless marriages,
For pizza, bowling, malls, and credit cards—
And all our lazy ways and fears and guilt—
And know that that is all there ever is.

She steps back into the crowd; a man steps forth.

MAN. She thought to be so haughty and demanding,
That men must stride on mountains at her side.
But now she'll be the easy toy of all.
They'll use her body anytime they please.

JUSTINE. They say that men in millions everywhere
But longed to meet the challenge I threw down.
My body was a symbol of the joy
With which a woman can reward a man.

MAN. We longed to feel what any man would feel
In taking you, but never thought that we
Could rise to that. That's what excites us so
In stories of some proud and lovely woman
Who's stripped and raped by prisoners and guards.
We wish they'd film your rape.

JUSTINE.   I'm not afraid.

The man steps back; another woman pushes forward.

WALTER DONWAY

SECOND WOMAN. The very thought that made us hate you!
If you'd but cry, and plead for clemency,
We'd love you once again, and even now
Petition very heaven in our prayers
To spare you from this fate.

JUSTINE.   I'm not afraid.

SECOND WOMAN. You must not say that, though, Justine. For all
Your loss of freedom, wealth, and privacy
Are nothing to us if you're not afraid.

JUSTINE. But people said I was a god to them.
Why do you wish your gods to be afraid?

SECOND WOMAN. But Christ cried out to God in his despair.
He died to save us from our sins, but you
Won't even ask forgiveness and be saved.
The prison's sure to break you, though; we'll know
That nobody is better than we are.
Are you afraid of *nothing?*

*Justine does not answer. The guards move her forward
toward the prison gate. She stops, looks at the crowd, and
speaks deliberately.*

JUSTINE.   I am afraid.
I'm afraid of you.

SECOND WOMAN.   Fear us? But we love all
The poor, and meek, and humble—and all
Of suffering mankind who seek our mercy.

TROUBADOUR. What can we know of Aphrodite
If we but gaze into the sky?
Our glory is to lift our eyes,
Although she never make reply.

JUSTINE. I'm so afraid. What love is there for me?

*The troubadour has reached the far right stage. He unties a string
from his guitar, drops the guitar, and moves nearer to Justine. He
walks at ease, but holds the string like a garrote.*
He leaps to face Justine.

JUSTINE. You!

*The guards react too slowly. He wraps the garrote around Jus-
tine's neck. His hands lock behind her neck. He falls backward,
pulling her on top of him.*

FIRST GUARD. Be quick! Release her! Save her! Save her!

The first guard struggles with the troubadour's locked hands. The second guard stands beside the two, gun drawn.

His hands! His hands are locked! Too strong! Kill him!

Second guard tries to aim the gun at the troubadour's head, but Justine's body is over him, and she bobs her head to block the gun.

SECOND GUARD. My God! She moves her head, protects him! If I shoot now, I could hit her!

FIRST REPORTER. The crowd is screaming, "Save her, save her!" They've rushed the guards to grab the gun!

SECOND GUARD. Stop, stop! You're doing nothing that can save her! Stop!

FIRST GUARD. She's isn't moving, I can shoot!

The guard fires. Both bodies on the ground are motionless in their embrace.

He's dead!

SECOND GUARD. But she's dead, too. It's late, too late, too late.

SECOND REPORTER. The crowd is going mad! The guards are fleeing!

FIRST REPORTER. And now the crowd cries: "Strip her! Strip her!"

The end

How Bad Values Undercut Progress

In bygone Wessex of fierce Cerdic's day,
The yearly hunt for unicorns could spoil
An otherwise glorious month of May.

A chieftain bold as even Cynnic found
He must attend to distant tribal turmoil
That time of year, and never was around.

The so-called volunteers were younger men,
Rehearsing battles over mugs of mead,
Suggesting that things haven't changed, since then.

The woods were green, with posies everywhere,
The morning they set off to do the deed;
A yearning young men feel was in the air.

None doubted the technology was known.
Each hunter donned a gold-and-purple vest,
And had a gong to strike with oxen bone.

Hearing the din, the beast would come to see,
And charge the colors of the royal crest.
The hunter placed himself before a tree.

Touched By Its Rays

He had to dodge, but must not dodge too soon.
The spiraling horn would stick in the wood;
The hunter could hope to live into June.

II

The only problem, as one fellow said,
Was no one ever caught a unicorn—
But look at all the hunters who were dead.

Well, springtime works its will with every man;
So they resolved to taste life's joys, that morn,
Before they gave their all for chief and clan.

Three maids all tender white were at their bath
Just where the river widened at the bend;
They shrieked to see the hunters on the path.

Yet, when the troop moved on, the merry three,
With tresses damp, and jesting without end,
Had cast their lots with that good company.

"We near the wood wherein the beast may hide,
And some, this day, will gaze upon his spear.
We pray to know a woman's warmth!" men cried.

WALTER DONWAY

"Our hearts cannot refuse a brave man's will,"
Liz sighed, "but pray you leave our Lily, here,
For she's but twelve and sweetly virgin, still."

Alas, but Lily scowled to see them go.
She dropped her garments; she did as she would,
Then dozed to dream what only she could know.

III

Contentment left the hunters sad and still,
Returning from a pleasant brook-side glade,
For now, all knew, they must do Cerdic's will.

Oh, how they stared to see an idea born:
The virgin lap, the chastely dozing maid,
The nestled head of the unicorn.

They marched in procession, banging the gong.
The unicorn came without any fuss,
Enchanted that Lily led it along.

Touched By Its Rays

At first the clan gathered and craned to look.
But marvels fade, and Cerdic was like us:
When all it took was taking, Cerdic took.

He severed the horn from the snow-white head,
And, later that night, ravished Lily, too.
The crimson dawn saw the unicorn dead.

The moral's hardly clear: Cerdic a brute?
The unicorn in love? A virgin who
Surely was pure, but didn't give a hoot?

It's plain the new technique did not permit
Cerdic to do his clan the slightest good;
His values, one concludes, weren't up to it.

The Fading Banner

The day we marched, the simple sun's untroubled face
Went beaming, just as though no dark, titanic clouds
Rode forth to sunder brotherhood and in its place
To pitch the blazing brand of war. The mocking crowds
Caught up the thoughtless cheer of the mild autumn day
And jeered our fading banner's earnest warning cry.
But how should we, who only know to kneel and pray
For peace, find words to move those boys who soon will die
But now can only leer as though at women led
Triumphal into Rome, the naked spoils of war?
O lend us words to sing the unconsidered dead,
Who in a year will fall in every field, and more
Who will be left to thrash upon the awful cot
Where sighs away the soul. Are we alone to see
That all the noble hopes and cherished safety sought
Through war are power's lies to insecurity?
The crowd at every turn now chants its faithful, brave,
Uncomprehending zeal, as though redeeming man
Were but a season's frolic and war could save
A nation, mere belief in freedom for a plan.
How will the hushed, unsparing voice of peace be heard
Above the mesmerizing pulse of martial passion
That throbs with threats and promises in every word
Now uttered by this man from Illinois, called Lincoln?

Touched By Its Rays

A Bitch Blew Into Town

Oh yes, New Orleans was a city
That had its special way of doing things.
At auctions in Hotel St. Louis
They bid on pretty octaroons:
But not with scars from being whipped,
Which showed she gave a master trouble.
Discerning buyers had her stripped.
Just step into the courtyard, sir.

The mighty Southern Babylon
Was pleased to take your cotton money
At any Storyville maison.
Perhaps you'd like a creole "niece"?
Or just a slave, who did the trick
A hundred times a day or more?
Out back, a gentleman could pick
A buck called Hercules or Ajax
And watch a fight that left someone
Out cold, his scrotum booted flat.
The old hands winked that half the fun
Was watching how the ladies stared.

My luck was seeing New Orleans
When I was young and it was there.
It taught me what the fellow means:
"You've got to see it while you can."
The week I went, they closed a den
On Bourbon Street, called Purple Rose,
Where nude young ladies squirmed for men,
Who sat above the little stage.
 A girl, it seems, advised some guy
To look, not touch, and this ole boy
Had come back with a gun to try
To get her pregnant with a bullet.

And that was just Big Easy's way,
Until a bitch they called Katrina
Blew into town and wouldn't play
The slave game, whore game, strip game.
This bitch kicked ass, this bitch took names;
She didn't stop till those ole boys
Forgot about the other dames
Just trying to keep their trousers dry.
Please draw comparisons with care;
This wasn't Sodom or Gomorrah
And big Katrina wasn't fair.
But hey, we're talking New Orleans.

Touched By Its Rays

An Old Flame

Alone this evening, I Google your name,
Then hesitate, reluctant, now, to see
Your **bold**, repetitious, digital fame:
This place wherein the world shares you with me.
One June, at dusk, I walked around your pond.
You loved this misty hour when the loon
Would laugh; you'd say the train's noise-ghost, beyond
The fields and piney hills, was coming soon.
I saw the path to where your cabin stood,
But wasn't it enough to linger here,
Where once the evenings spoke to you the good
Of things in sounds that yet might reach the ear?
In this blue dusk of my computer's glow
O let them speak, Henry David Thoreau.

WALTER DONWAY

The Fall
(For Roger)

Recall afternoons autumn perfect
In sun-soft nut-odorous air
And our shuffling golden-loaded
Steps or soft kicks till school and home
Never were but only yearning lost
And last as sky or Indian trails
Or grassy graves of white cities.
Did love's gravity weigh the heart
So and laden the air with hurt?
Or some dear unwhispered wish
Unvoiced unto the last star?

The Woods

What is this place, this pleasant shade?
Just here, the shining wake that passing
Left on the sunny field of hay
Meets this path long use has made.

What is this tumbled shack, I see?
Its bleachy boards were darker once,
And now just half its door still swings.
But how, how can this ever be?

That little brook! It pauses where
A pool has formed about that rock,
Sloped and smooth as a kindly back.
Should not two boys be sitting there?

What is this place, this brooding wood?
Four corners at two crossing paths
Present a scene so singular,
There's but one place that ever could.

How came I to this boyhood spot—
Long gone, long gone, these many years?
For love can clutch a memory
But journey to it just in thought.

Ah, now I think I can recall:
I heard soft voices all around,
Though sad, and far, as taking leave—
And then I heard no one at all.